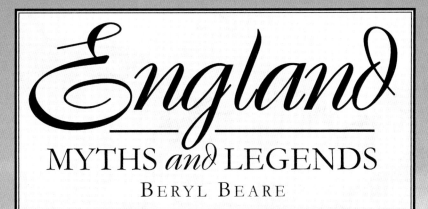

England

MYTHS and LEGENDS

BERYL BEARE

England

MYTHS and LEGENDS

Beryl Beare

For Sue and Duncan

Right: The Houses of Parliament – a potent symbol of England's rich history of legend and folklore.

This is a Parragon Book

First published in Great Britain in 1996 by
Parragon
Queen Street House
4-5 Queen Street
Bath BA1 1HE United Kingdom

Designed and produced by
Stonecastle Graphics Limited
Old Chapel Studio, Plain Road, Marden,
Tonbridge, Kent TN12 9LS United Kingdom

© Parragon Books Limited 1996
Reprinted 1999

ISBN 0-75252-978-1

Printed in Italy

Photographic credits:
(Abbreviations: r = right, l = left, t = top, b = below)

Telegraph Colour Library: 2-3, 5, 7, 8*(b)*, 9, 11*(inset)*, 12*(t)*, 15*(l)*, 15*(r)*, 16-17*(t)*, 17*(b)*, 18-19, 20-21, 22*(tl)*, 23*(inset)*, 24*(l)*, 26-27, 29*(r)*, 30-31, 33*(l)*, 35, 36*(l)*, 36*(r)*, 37, 38-39, 48*(l)*, 51, 53, 54-55, 56*(l)*, 56-57, 58*(l)*, 60*(t)*, 60*(br)*, 61, 62*(l)*, 64*(inset)*, 65*(r)*, 68-69*(t)*, 68-69*(b)*, 70-71, 72, 74-75, 76.

Greg Evans International: 1, 8*(t)*, 10, 11*(r)*, 12*(b)*, 13*(l)*, 13*(r)*, 14*(t)*, 16*(l)*, 16*(r)*, 17*(t)*, 19*(inset)*, 19*(b)*, 21*(t)*, 22*(b)*, 23*(b)*, 24-25, 25*(l)*, 26*(l)*, 28*(l)*, 28*(inset)*, 31*(r)*, 34, 39*(r)*, 40-41, 41*(t)*, 41*(b)*, 44, 45*(r)*, 48-49, 50*(inset)*, 50-51, 57*(r)*, 58-59, 59*(inset)*, 59*(r)*, 60*(l)*, 62*(r)*, 63, 64-65, 66*(l)*, 66*(r)*, 67, 68*(l)*, 71*(r)*, 73, 77, 79.

The Image Bank: 6, 14*(b)*, 20*(inset)*, 22*(inset)*, 27*(t)*, 32, 33*(r)*, 42-43, 43*(r)*, 45*(l)*, 49*(r)*, 50*(b)*, 55*(r)*.

Colorific!: 46*(inset)*, 46-47, 47*(r)*, 74*(l)*.

Touchstone: 28-29, 52, 78*(inset)*, 78.

Images Colour Library Limited: 75*(r)*.

The author would like to thank:

Sharon Bleasdale, North West Tourist Board,
    Wigan
Susan E Teed, Yorkshire & Humberside Tourist
    Board, York
Louise Wood, London Tourist Board
PR Department, HM Tower of London
The South East England Tourist Board,
    Tunbridge Wells, for *Princess Pocahontas* (p 30)
The Heart of England Tourist Board,
    Worcester, for *The North-South Grave* (p 61)
Chester City Council Tourism Development
    Unit and **Haunted Chester** by Rupert
    Matthews for *A Romantic Roman* (p 62) and
    The Invisible Ghost (p 63).
Sue Henderson, City of Sunderland Tourism
    Development and **The Lambton Worm** by
    Keith Armstrong for *The Lambton Worm* (p 79)
Lancashire Hill Country, Blackburn Tourist
    Information Centre; The Borough of
    Pendle, and **The Witches of Pendle** by Paul
    Barlow, for *The Witches of Pendle* (pp 76-77)
and special thanks to Anne Jenkins of The
English Tourist Board, Hammersmith, London.

Contents

Introduction
Page 6

West Country Legends
Page 8

The Summer Lands
Page 14

The Cradle of a Nation
Page 20

Legends of the South East
Page 26

Legends of London
Page 32

The Home Counties
Page 38

East Anglia and the Fens
Page 42

Legends of the Shires
Page 50

Legends of the Heartland
Page 60

Lakeland Legends
Page 68

Legends of the North
Page 72

Index & Place Names
Page 80

Introduction

ENGLAND is renowned for her 'infinite variety'. And so it is with her folklore. From the thriving hub of the historic capital to the desolate moors of Devonshire; from a haunted 'Heartland' city to the northern lakes of Cumbria – there is always something interesting to catch the eye, something unexpected to capture the imagination.

Cornwall, in the West Country, offers not only the timeless tales of King Arthur, but also evidence of the more recent past. The gaunt, castle-like ruins of engine houses and chimney-stacks; monuments to an age when men burrowed beneath the cliffs and moors in search of tin and copper – and reminders of the ghosts and fears that haunted them.

On Dartmoor, granite tors rise above bogs and rolling moorland. A scene that prepares us for the demon dogs that haunt the area – and warns us, perhaps, that the Wild Hunt could be close behind!

Across the country to the once water-logged Fens, where we meet the kings and heroes of the past. Here, also, we may chance upon the mysteriously frightening Jack-o'-Lanterns of the marshes. Then inland and up-country to encounter fairies and boggarts, haunted caves and stone circles, witches, giants and murderers.

Now, almost at the dawn of the 21st century, we may think we can afford to be sceptical about such stories. But we are often closer to the fears and superstitions of our forefathers than we realize – and our heritage goes back a long way.

Many of the English roads appear to twist and turn aimlessly, but in fact there is a purpose to their erratic behaviour. They bend to avoid some ancient fort or castle, a wayside grave, a healing spring – or perhaps the site of a gallows.

The 17th century witch-hunts are no more, but witches still haunt the Hill Country of Lancashire. Mother Shipton is long dead, but her cave is still there to visit. The legends and myths of England are not only great in number and variety, but also accessible. Whether the story is of saint, king or monster, there is nearly always something to be seen. The Tourist Boards are very helpful in this respect, and always happy to give further information.

So folklore thrives – but what of the fairies? The bustle of modern life may have sent them away for good. Central heating will certainly have driven them from the home, for domestic fairies were said to live in the hearth. But if you still have a fireplace in your house, then who knows . . .

Below: The ghostly ruins of Sham Castle, Staffordshire.
Right: A haunting West Country seascape.

West Country Legends

The 'Beast of Bodmin'

Bodmin Moor, Cornwall

NOT ALL legends are from the past. The notorious 'Beast of Bodmin' is a living legend – or perhaps a living fact. There have been a number of reported 'sightings' of the creature, and one farmer greets visitors with a notice on his gate that states: 'Wild Big Cats. Keep Out'.

'Beast of Bodmin' believers were recently excited by the discovery of a leopard's skull on the moor. But expert examination revealed that it was almost certainly once attached to a leopard skin rug.

Dozmary Pool

Bodmin Moor, Cornwall

ON Bodmin Moor there is a great tarn called Dozmary Pool, one of several places associated with King Arthur's sword, Excalibur.

According to legend, Arthur commanded one of his knights to throw the sword into the pool. Reluctantly, the knight obeyed, whereupon a hand rose from the water, caught the sword by its jewelled hilt and drew it under.

In the 17th century, the ghost of a cruel magistrate named Tregeagle (pronounced Tregayle) was condemned to toil at impossible tasks. One of the tasks was to empty Dozmary Pool with a leaky limpet shell. In 1859 the pool dried up – but if Tregeagle's ghost was responsible, it had certainly laboured a long time for results!

The Lovers

Castle Dore, St Sampson, Cornwall

KING Mark of Cornwall had a court at Castle Dore in the sixth century. One day, the king picked up a long golden hair dropped by a swallow, and said he would marry only the maiden to whom the hair belonged. He charged his nephew, Tristan, to search for her.

Tristan discovered her in Ireland. She was Iseult (or Isolde), the beautiful daughter of the Irish king. He took her back to Cornwall with him, but on the journey they drank a love potion intended for King Mark's wedding night, and fell passionately in love.

Iseult married King Mark but even after the effects of the potion wore off, she and Tristan continued to love each other deeply. The king heard of a meeting planned between the two and decided to spy on them. He hid himself in a tree – but the lovers saw his reflection in a pool, and by talking together casually managed to allay his suspicions.

Tristan married a Breton girl but never ceased to love Iseult. Grieving for her brought about his death, and an ancient stone cross marks his grave at Castle Dore.

Far left, top: Mysterious prehistoric stone monuments are a common sight in Cornwall.
Far left, below: Since the dawn of time, the sea has shaped Cornwall's destiny – and many of its legends.
Left: St Michael's Mount is silhouetted against a dramatic Cornish sunset.

The Lost Land

Land's End, Cornwall

SMUGGLING was rife on this rocky part of the coast in the 18th century. Prussia Cove, near Land's End, got its name by being the secret harbour of a notorious smuggler known as 'The King of Prussia'.

Long before this, however, Land's End was said to be the entrance to Lyonesse – a fertile land stretching to the Isles of Scilly. Midway between Land's End and Scilly is a group of rocks, the 'Seven Stones', believed by some to be all that remains of Lyonesse.

The Cornish people call the area bounded by these rocks *Tregva* – 'a dwelling'. There were once reports of windows and pieces of furniture surfacing here, and the roofs of houses being glimpsed beneath the waves.

In the 11th century Lyonesse was suddenly drowned by the sea and only one man managed to escape. His name was Trevilian, and he cheated death by leaping on his white horse and galloping ahead of the waves.

Today, the Trevilian family arms show the likeness of a horse rising from the sea, to commemorate the event. And earlier this century there were still fishermen who swore that they had seen drowned buildings around the Seven Stones lighthouse.

Merlin's Rock

Mousehole, Cornwall

MERLIN'S fame as a prophet survives at the coastal village of Mousehole – pronounced 'Mouzel'. In 1595 the town was burnt to the ground by troops from three Spanish ships, and only one building survived.

Merlin's Rock stands near the quay, and the Spanish attack was regarded locally as the fulfilment of the wizard's prophecy, which stated:

There shall land on the Rock of Merlin,
Those who shall burn Paul, Penzance and
Newlyn.

Not all of Merlin's prophecies have been fulfilled, however. He also said that:

When the Rame Head and Dodman meet
Men and women will have cause to weep.

But the cause for this weeping remains undisclosed, as the two headlands are still 40 miles apart!

Mevagissey Duck

Mevagissey, Cornwall

MEVAGISSEY was established in the Middle Ages, but developed later when it became known for its pilchards. The Royal Navy used to refer to the tiny fish as 'Mevagissey Duck'.

In the Porthilly area of Mevagissey is a church with no bells and only a tiny tower – facts which are derided in a local rhyme:

You men of Porthilly, why are you so silly
In having so little power?
You sold every bell, as Gorran men tell,
For money to pull down your tower!

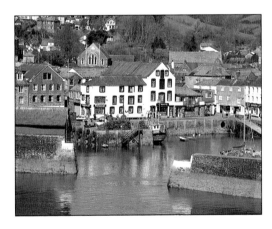

Far left and inset: The rugged coast of Land's End was a favourite haunt of smugglers for many centuries.
Above: Since the Middle Ages, Mevagissey has been a busy fishing village – famous for its 'Mevagissey Duck'.

The Knockers

St Just, Cornwall

THE 'knockers' were fairy miners who inhabited the tin mines of Cornwall. It was said they were the spirits of people who had lived in Cornwall before the Celts, and were neither good enough for heaven, nor bad enough for hell.

They were called knockers because of the sounds they made as they laboured at the metal lodes, or veins – and they often brought good luck to the miners by leading them to the richest veins. However, like all fairies they could be vindictive if upset. And nothing upset them so much as having no fuggan (Cornish cake) left out by a miner for them to feast on.

A miner from St Just called Tom Trevorrow was working at Ballowal Mine. One day, he heard the knockers at work and told them to be quiet and go away. Immediately, he was struck by a shower of small stones. He took no notice and after a while heard the knockers crying:

Tom Trevorrow! Tom Trevorrow!
Leave some of thy fuggan for Knocker
Or bad luck to thee tomorrow.

Tom became angry and cursed the knockers. When they next spoke they, too, sounded angry.

Tommy Trevorrow, Tommy Trevorrow!
We'll send thee bad luck tomorrow,
Thou old curmudgeon, to eat all thy fuggan
And leave not a morsel for Knocker.

The following day, Tom found a rock-fall had buried his tools and the vein of ore he had been working on. After that, bad luck seemed to dog him every day – until he was forced to leave the mine and become a farm labourer.

King Arthur's Birthplace

Tintagel, Cornwall

ACCORDING to local legend, Arthur was born at Tintagel Castle, fathered by King Uther Pendragon.

King Uther fell passionately in love with Ygerna, the beautiful wife of Gorlois, Duke of Cornwall. She was safely immured in Tintagel Castle while Gorlois set out to defend his land against Uther's troops. But Uther was so obsessed by her that he was unable to concentrate on the battle.

The magician, Merlin, produced a potion that turned Uther into an exact replica of Ygerna's husband, Gorlois. Disguised so effectively, Uther found it easy to gain access to the castle and have his way with the lady.

King Arthur was conceived that night, and Gorlois also fell in battle. Later, resuming his real appearance, Uther married Ygerna.

Far left and inset: The remains of abandoned tin mines can be seen scattered across Cornwall – perhaps some are still inhabited by 'knockers'.

Below left: The ruined walls of ancient Tintagel Castle, the legendary birthplace of King Arthur.

Below: Tintagel Cove – possibly both King Uther Pendragon and his son, King Arthur, admired this view.

The Summer Lands

Bladud and the Swine

Bath, Avon

THE waters of the Roman spa of *Aquae Sulis* – Bath as we know it today – were discovered by Bladud, son of the legendary King Lud of Britain. Prince Bladud contracted leprosy and was banished from his father's court. His mother, the queen, wept at his departure and told him that he could return if he should ever be cured.

Bladud found work as a swineherd, but before long the swine he cared for also caught leprosy. Fearing their owner's wrath, he drove them across the River Avon – at a place that is still called Swineford.

Agitated and in pain, the diseased animals panicked and plunged into an evil smelling bog in the valley. Bladud struggled until he was almost too exhausted to continue, but eventually he managed to haul them out.

To his amazement he discovered that they were no longer leprous. He immersed himself in the warm, muddy water and found that he, too, was cured.

Right and inset: The famous medicinal Roman spring waters of Bath, discovered by the leper Prince Bladud.

Overjoyed, he returned home to the court. He then arranged for wells to be sunk into the bog, and the healing waters that were harnessed became the medicinal springs of Bath that are famous today.

Fairy Haunts

Black Down Hills, Somerset

A LONG time ago, the fairies used to hold a fair on the Black Down Hills. They were also abroad there at other times, but their activities were seldom witnessed by mortals – because they never showed themselves to those who went in search of them.

However, a school master who was once walking on the Black Down Hills at twilight, happened on a fairy ring by chance. He said he saw a number of fairies going round and round, singing and 'making all manner of small odd noises'.

The making of strange little noises is typical of fairy behaviour. In the 17th century a Mr Lilly met what he took to be a fairy, and asked if it was a good spirit or a bad one. He said there was no reply, but that the 'fairy' disappeared with a 'curious perfume and most melodious twang'.

Buckland St Mary, a short distance from the Black Down Hills, is the last place in Somerset where the 'red-clothed' fairies were seen. It is said that they fought a pitched battle with the pixies – and lost. So everywhere west of the River Parret is now Pixieland.

Above: The early morning light casts a mysterious hue over Dunkery Beacon, Exmoor.
Right: It is not difficult to imagine discovering a fairy ring in this beautiful Somerset landscape.

Arthur's Hill

Cadbury Castle, near Yeovil, Somerset

THE HILL-fort known as Cadbury Castle above the village of South Cadbury is, in fact, Camelot. This was King Arthur's headquarters in the sixth century, and it was from here – Cadbury-Camelot – that he led the Britons to victory against the Saxon invaders.

No one reigned at Camelot before Arthur, and no one has reigned there since. But the hill is reputed to be hollow, and he and his knights are said to lie there sleeping – until such time as England shall call upon them again.

Arthur sleeps in a cavern closed with great iron gates, and on one night of the year – some say Midsummer Eve – the gates stand open and he can be seen inside. Every so often, the ghosts of King Arthur and his knights take a nocturnal ride over the hilltop and down to Sutton Montis. Here, it is said, the horses drink at a spring.

However, it is by no means easy to catch this spectral ride, for it may take place on Midsummer Eve, Midsummer Night or Christmas Eve. Then again, it may happen only once every seventh year!

The Wish Hounds

Dartmoor, Devon

WISTMAN'S Wood on Dartmoor is an ancient copse of gnarled and stunted oaks. In the 19th century it was associated with the Wish Hounds – the phantom Black Dogs that are reputed to haunt Dartmoor, and were the inspiration for Sir Arthur Conan Doyle's *The Hound of the Baskervilles*.

The Wish Hounds run with the Wild Hunt, led by a spectral huntsman who – some say – has dealings with the Devil.

One dark night, a Dartmoor farmer was riding home from Widdicombe Fair by way of Hamel Down. As he passed a circle of standing stones, a pack of phantom hounds rushed silently past him, urged on by a dark huntsman.

'What sport have you had?' the farmer called out to the strange rider, and then jokingly asked for some of his game.

'This is for you!' the huntsman replied, and tossed him a well-wrapped bundle. Gratified, the farmer caught it, but was unable to see what was in it until he got home.

He then unwrapped the bundle carefully, by the light of a lantern. To his horror, he found that it contained the lifeless body of his own child.

All pictures: A county of infinite beauty and variety, Devon boasts the wild splendour of Dartmoor, rugged tors, prehistoric stone circles and a magnificent coastline – all steeped in ancient myths and legends.

Arthur at Avalon

Glastonbury, Somerset

MORTALLY injured at the battle of Camlann in Cornwall, King Arthur was borne away to the the Isle of Avalon, the 'Isle of Apples', to be cured of his wounds. Avalon was one of the Celtic 'Otherworld' islands, and in the 12th century – some 600 years after Arthur's last battle – it came to be associated with Glastonbury.

Arthur was reputedly buried at Glastonbury Abbey. In 1190, the Norman King Henry II gave orders for the grave to be excavated. Seven feet down a lead cross was discovered, inscribed with the words: 'Here lies buried the renowned King Arthur in the Isle of Avalon'.

Nine feet below the cross was a great coffin made of oak, and inside was the skeleton of a tall man. There were also some slighter bones and a scrap of yellow hair that may have belonged to Guinevere.

However, the tradition of the 'once-and-future King' was not diminished by these findings. Many people still believe Arthur to be sleeping – if not at Cadbury-Camelot, then in some other cave or hill. As the *Black Book of Carmarthen* has it: 'Concealed till Doomsday is the grave of Arthur'!

Right and inset: Two views of Glastonbury Tor, the enchanted area of Somerset often associated with the legend of King Arthur.

The Witch of Wookey

Wookey Hole, near Wells, Somerset

𝒜 STALAGMITE in the famous Wookey Hole caves is known as the Witch of Wookey. Long ago, she lived in the caves with her two familiars – a goat and its kid.

Although she was wicked and spiteful, she had not always been that way. It was said she had once been crossed in love and that ever since she had shown vindictiveness to all the villagers of Wookey, and was especially spiteful to lovers.

A local monk had taken holy vows after the witch had spoilt his own romance. He had planned to marry a girl from Wookey, but the witch had put a spell on their forthcoming wedding and wrecked it.

When the people of Wookey appealed to the Abbot of Glastonbury to rid them of the witch, this particular monk was sent to the cave to confront her.

As soon as she saw him, she tried to flee. But he managed to sprinkle her with holy water and she was instantly turned to stone. And there she stands to this day, petrified on the bank of the River Axe in the Great Cave at Wookey Hole.

Left: The ruins of the once magnificent Glastonbury Abbey, where the grave of King Arthur was excavated in 1190, on the orders of King Henry II.

The Cradle of a Nation

The Mystery Stones

Avebury Stone Circles, Wiltshire

ON A misty autumn morning the great stone circle of Avebury seems to consist of brooding stone ghosts. And perhaps that is just what they are; the natural shapes of these unhewn rocks seem to suggest male and female figures.

What, exactly, was their purpose? Were they dedicated to serpent worship, as was originally supposed? Or do they – as is now believed – form an open temple where fertility rites were once performed?

By all accounts, some of those rites were quite horrendous. At one time, pilgrims came from all over Britain to Avebury, for ceremonies which were said to include ritual sacrifices and cannibalism. During the Middle Ages the Church became alarmed at the revival of the pagan rites, and orders were given for the stones to be buried.

In the 1930s a man's skeleton was discovered under one of the stones. With him were found several coins and surgical tools, identifying him as a surgeon-barber who died in about 1300. He was thought to have been killed when the stone – which he was helping to bury – fell on him.

During the 17th and 18th centuries, farmers used many of the remaining stones for building houses and walls. However, most were recovered earlier this century in an attempt to restore the 'temple' to its original form.

The 'Negative' Ghost

*B*ISHAM Abbey in Berkshire has a celebrated ghost, but it haunts the abbey in a most unusual way. Lady Elizabeth Hoby's ghostly apparition takes the form of a photographic negative – the dark parts appearing light and the light parts, such as the face, appearing dark. The reason for this anomaly has never been explained.

Lady Hoby lived in the 16th century and was a personal friend of Queen Elizabeth. She was learned and domineering, and intolerant of those less able than herself.

She beat her young son William over and over again, simply because he could not write without making blots. Eventually she beat him to death, and her remorse was so great that, in negative form, she continues to haunt the room where the tragedy occurred.

Far left and inset: The great stone circle at Avebury, where ritual sacrifices and cannibalism may have taken place in ancient times.
Above left: St Michael's church in the village of Bray.

The 'Vicar of Bray'

Bray, Berkshire

*T*HE REAL vicar of Bray was probably Simon Alleyn. He became vicar there in 1551 and continued in that calling through the reigns of Edward VI, Mary and Elizabeth.

The vicar was renowned for his religious inconsistency; he was first a papist, then became a protestant, then a papist – and then a protestant again. However, he denied being a 'turn-coat', saying 'I always kept my principle . . . to live and die the Vicar of Bray.'

The King and the Witch

The Rollright Stones, Cotswolds, Oxfordshire

MORE than 2000 years ago a king set out with his army to conquer England. At Rollright Hill, on the borders of Oxfordshire and Warwickshire, he met a witch who told him that if he could see Long Compton after taking seven strides, he would be King of England.

Knowing Long Compton to be just over the brow of the hill, the king strode forward confidently. But a mound rose up in front of him and the witch exclaimed:

Rise up stick, and stand still stone,
For King of England thou shalt be none;
As Long Compton thou ne'er didst see
Thou and thy men hoar stones shall be.

Stones they instantly became – and stones they remain. The mound (much reduced by ploughing) can still be seen in front of the 'King Stone'. There are said to be 72 stones in the circle, but legend maintains that no one shall live who counts the stones three times and finds the number the same.

Nearby stand the Whispering Knights, a smaller group of the king's men also turned to stone. They are now regarded as oracles and will occasionally 'whisper' the future to visitors.

Far left: The beautiful patchwork landscape of the Cotswolds is rich with ancient myths and legends.
Left: Who dares to count the stones that form the ancient circle on Rollright Hill? Perhaps it is safer to listen to the oracle of the Whispering Knights (inset).
Below and inset right: The magnificent stone circle of Stonehenge may have been a temple or even a primitive computer for calculating the movement of the stars.

The Giant's Dance

Stonehenge, Salisbury Plain, Wiltshire

STONEHENGE is more than 4000 years old, yet still we have little idea how it was constructed. And what was its purpose? A temple dedicated to sun worship? An ancient 'computer' for calculating the movement of heavenly bodies? Or do the Bronze Age barrows and deposits of human bones found in the vicinity suggest a funeral monument?

This is what Geoffrey of Monmouth, the 12th century author, believed. According to him, Aurelius, a king of the Britons, wanted to build a monument over the graves of hundreds of British noblemen who had been massacred by the Saxons.

The king summoned Merlin, the magician, who told him that in Ireland there stood a circle of huge stones called the Giants' Dance. They had been brought from Africa by giants long ago and were used in religious rites – and also had special healing properties.

Aurelius sent an army to fetch the stones, but all their attempts to shift them were in vain. Merlin then placed in position his own gear of 'engines and other contrivances' and dismantled the circle.

The stones were loaded aboard ships, transported to Britain and brought to the burial site, where Aurelius conducted a ceremony. Merlin reconstructed the circle on Salisbury Plain, where it became the Stonehenge that we know today.

The Moonrakers

Swindon, Wiltshire

A FEW hundred years ago, Dutch and Flemish merchants – attracted by the fine Wiltshire wool – had their headquarters in Swindon. Their only complaint was the heavy import duty imposed on their favourite drink, Hollands gin.

The Wiltshiremen realized that a restriction on the beverage could affect their profitable trading with the merchants. So they met together to find an answer to the problem.

Their solution was to set up a highly efficient smuggling organization. Barrels of the spirits were landed in secluded coves on the Hampshire coast and brought to Swindon by night. During the daytime the barrels were hidden in village ponds and meadows, and then removed from their hiding places after dark.

One moonlit night, the smugglers were raking their barrels out of a pond when they were surprised by patrolling Excisemen. The 'rakers' immediately feigned rustic simplicity and, pointing to the moon and then to its reflection in the water, told the officials that a piece of it had fallen into the pond and they were trying to rake it out.

The Excisemen laughed at such foolishness and rode on their way. And Wiltshiremen have been known as 'Moonrakers' ever since.

Below: The early morning mist heralds a new day – and perhaps, a new legend.
Right: Autumn colours enhance a quiet corner of Windsor Great Park.
Far right: Windsor Castle.

Herne the Hunter

Windsor, Berkshire

WINDSOR Great Park is haunted by Herne the Hunter. In times of national crisis he has sometimes been seen standing by a great oak tree – Herne's Oak – that grew in the park.

Today if he appears, it is usually on horseback, sometimes blowing his hunting horn for added effect – although Herne himself must be a daunting sight, festooned with chains and with a stag's antlers growing out of his brow. According to legend, he was once a royal huntsman who saved the life of a king by placing himself between the monarch and a wounded stag. Herne received the full impact of the stag's antlers and was mortally wounded.

The king summoned a magician, who told him the only way to save Herne's life was to cut off the stag's antlers and tie them to the huntsman's brow. This was done and Herne recovered, and for many years continued to serve the king and enjoy his favour.

However, the other huntsmen became jealous of Herne's influence and eventually persuaded the king to dismiss him. This so distressed Herne that he hanged himself from a tree, and has haunted the Great Park ever since.

Princess Pocahontas

Gravesend, Kent

IN 1608, Captain John Smith was captured by Algonkin Indians and brought before Powhaten, a native American chief, who sentenced him to death. Smith was the founding father of America's first permanent English colony in Virginia and Princess Pocahontas, the chief's daughter, pleaded for his life. But her father refused the plea.

Just as the executioner's blow was about to fall, the young princess threw herself across John Smith's body and saved him. Her brave deed caused her father to relent, and the prisoner was released. He eventually returned to England, wounded, and Pocahontas was heartbroken.

She remained with the English settlers – who may have held her against her will – and in 1613 became a Christian. The following year she married John Rolfe, an English tobacco trader, and two years afterwards accompanied him to England.

Her visit was a great success – she was even received at court. But before long she became ill and it was decided she should return to Virginia.

She did not make the journey, however, but died at Gravesend where she is buried – the first American to be buried in England. Her statue now stands outside St George's church, in the Princess Pocahontas Gardens.

Right and far right: West Sussex – a land fit for dragons.

Knucker Hole

Lyminster, West Sussex

THE Lyminster Knucker was a fearsome dragon who lived in a bottomless pool near the church. It ravaged the countryside and devoured cattle, men and maidens. Particularly maidens, for they were the Knucker's favourite fare.

Soon the region was almost bereft of damsels, and those bachelors who had not already been eaten marched to the palace and complained to the King of Sussex. The king had an attractive daughter, and because of the dragon's voracious appetite he had kept her locked up in the castle. Now he offered her in marriage to anyone who could kill the Knucker.

A passing knight errant took up the challenge. He was not unduly brave, but wandering about had become tiring and he wanted to give up errantry and settle in one place. So he killed the dragon, married the princess and stayed happily at home in the palace.

Some folk reported that the dragon fought ferociously, but a more unkind version hinted that the knight paid a local baker to make a leaden cake which he fed to the dragon; the beast was then unable to rise to its feet.

A medieval tombstone, now inside the church, once marked the knight's grave.

Legends of London

Baker Street

Central London

ONE of London's most famous addresses never existed. Sherlock Holmes shared rooms with Dr John Watson at 221B Baker Street – but only in the stories created by Sir Arthur Conan Doyle.

Holmes, the extraordinary sleuth who reached conclusions by observing trifles, first appeared in *A Study in Scarlet* in 1887. The most famous of the Sherlock Holmes stories, *The Hound of the Baskervilles* was made into no less than seven films – the first in 1917.

However, those looking for the Baker Street address in vain can still find a shrine to the great detective. The sitting room of 221B has been faithfully reproduced at the Sherlock Holmes public house in Northumberland Street, Charing Cross.

The Bank of England

Central London

THE Bank of England has been known as 'The Old Lady of Threadneedle Street' since the end of the 18th century. The name was born from a cartoon published in 1797, in which William Pitt – who had given instructions for the issue of unlimited paper currency – was portrayed making advances to an elderly lady who represented the Bank.

Some years later the name was applied to a woman called Sarah Whitehead, whose brother Philip had been dismissed from the Bank on a charge of forgery. He was found guilty of the charge and executed in 1811.

Sarah was so unhinged by her brother's death that she appeared at the Bank every day for the next 25 years, asking for him. Upon her own death, she was buried in the old churchyard that later became a part of the Bank's gardens. Her ghost is said to have been seen in the vicinity on a number of occasions.

Left: The Sherlock Holmes public house, which features the great detective's sitting room of 221B Baker Street.

Westminster Abbey

Central London

KING Henry IV was reputed to have died in the Jerusalem chamber of Westminster Abbey – the unexpected fulfilment of a prophecy that he would 'die in Jerusalem'. Ironically, he had been taken ill while visiting the Abbey on the eve of his departure for the Holy Land.

The Stone of Scone – on which 34 successive Scottish kings were crowned – is now in Westminster Abbey, beneath the Coronation Chair. And the Abbey can lay claim to a number of ghosts. When it was built in 816AD, an apparition of St Peter himself was said to have appeared on the premises.

Above: 'The Old Lady of Threadneedle Street'.
Left: Westminster Abbey, haunt of a number of ghosts.

Dick Whittington and Miss Puss

Highgate Hill, London

DICK Whittington was a poor boy who lived in the reign of Edward III, and heard that the streets of London were paved with gold. He determined to make his way there and seek his fortune, but he found no gold and had to accept employment in the kitchen of a rich merchant, Mr Fitzwarren.

Dick worked hard but was scolded all day long by the cook. His nights were none too comfortable either, for the attic in which he slept was plagued by mice. So, for the price of one penny, Dick bought a cat.

He called her Miss Puss, and not only did she rid his attic of mice but her companionship made his life bearable. When he heard her purr he could almost accept the fact that he would never be able to afford to marry Alice, the merchant's daughter.

Mr Fitzwarren had a ship about to sail and asked his servants if they wanted a stake in the voyage. Dick's only possession was his beloved cat – but the captain promised to take care of her if she proved a good ratter, and Dick knew Miss Puss would do them both credit.

The ship sailed away to Barbary, where the captain heard that the king's palace was overrun with rats. He took Miss Puss to the palace and she dispatched the rats in no time. The grateful king bought the ship's cargo for a huge sum of money, and Miss Puss for ten times as much again!

Back in London, Dick found the cook's bullying impossible to bear without Miss Puss to comfort him, and decided to run away. He got as far as Highgate Hill, and sat down on a stone to rest. At that moment he heard the bells of Bow church ringing, and he was sure they said,

Turn again, Whittington,
Lord Mayor of London.

So he turned back, and soon afterwards Mr Fitzwarren's ship returned with news that Dick was a wealthy man. Now, at last, he could propose to Alice Fitzwarren. She accepted him and, as everyone knows, he did become Lord Mayor of London – not once, but thrice.

Far away, in the king's palace, Miss Puss lived a life of luxury. And when she gave birth to six lovely kittens the king, with due decorum, renamed her Mrs Puss.

You can still see the Whittington Stone on Highgate Hill, surmounted by the figure of Dick's cat.

Below: The colourful pageantry of the Lord Mayor's Show.
Right: A dramatic view of the Houses of Parliament.

The Tower of London

The City of London

THE Tower of London is famous for its history, hauntings – and past horrors. Medieval torture instruments included a diabolical device known as the 'Scavenger's Daughter', which compressed the victim's body into a ball.

Sir Walter Raleigh was imprisoned in the Tower for much of King James's reign. Yet he managed to grow tobacco plants and write his influential *History of the World*.

Princess Elizabeth – the future Queen Elizabeth I – was imprisoned in an upper room of the Bell Tower and interrogated about plots against her half-sister, Mary. She was released after two months but – understandably – retained a lasting dislike for the Tower.

What is now the 'Bloody Tower' originally controlled the watergate and was known as the Garden Tower. It is reputed to be where the two princes were murdered – hence the change of name.

What really happened to the two young sons of Edward IV remains a mystery. Richard Duke of Gloucester – later King Richard III – was their protector. The children were lodged in the Tower following their father's death in 1483, and day by day began to be seen less frequently behind the bars and windows.

In 1674 the skeletons of two children were discovered in a wooden chest during demolition work at the Tower. The bones were declared to be the correct size for the two boys, and King Charles II had them interred in Westminster Abbey.

The Crown Jewels

The City of London

IN THE 15th century, Mr Edwards and his wife, the guardians of the crown jewels, would show them to visitors for a fee. They were kept in the lower room of the Martin Tower. Visitors would be taken into the room, the door closed and the jewels removed from a cupboard.

However, following Colonel Blood's notorious attempt to steal the jewels, the procedure was changed and security tightened.

First ingratiating himself to Mr and Mrs Edwards in the guise of a clergyman, Blood then returned shortly afterwards with three companions. Unsuspectingly, Mr Edwards took them all downstairs to the lower room, where he was struck with a mallet and gagged.

The thieves, having hidden various larger pieces of the Regalia about their persons, were about to flee when Mr Edwards's son arrived home unexpectedly and raised the alarm. Three of the conspirators were caught, and the jewels were recovered.

Far left: The Tower of London by both night and day. Left: The lights of the majestic Tower Bridge shimmer their reflection in the silky darkness of the River Thames.

The Home Counties

Piers Shonks and the Dragon

Brent Pelham, Hertfordshire

A DRAGON lived at Brent Pelham in the 11th century, and he was a servant to the Devil. Many dragons were, of course, but the Devil was particularly fond of this one.

It had its lair under a yew tree and, in the manner of all dragons, it was very fierce and terrorized the district.

Piers Shonks, the lord of the manor, decided that it was his duty to destroy the beast. So he clad himself in full armour, took up his sword and spear and called his three fleet-footed hounds to heel. Then he set off for the yew tree.

After a fierce battle with the dragon Shonks thrust his sword down its throat and destroyed it. Immediately, the Devil appeared – furious at the loss of his servant – and swore to have Shonks' soul whether he was buried within the church or without.

Shonks managed to cheat the Devil, however. Before he died he shot an arrow at Brent Pelham church, to strike the wall north of the nave. There his tomb was built – neither within the church nor without – and there it can still be seen today.

The Trapdoor Murders

Colnbrook, Buckinghamshire

Below and below right: Despite the tranquil appearance of the rural Home Counties, its myths and legends tell tales of dark deeds and brutal murder.

THE Ostrich Inn at Colnbrook lays claim to being one of England's several 'oldest inns'. It is said to date from 1106, and to have been a resting place for King John on his journey to Runnymede to sign Magna Carta.

The most sinister story concerns the Jarmans, who ran the Ostrich in medieval times and had perfected a gruesome means of murdering wealthy visitors. When the victim was asleep, the husband would release a trapdoor concealed beneath the bed. The unfortunate sleeper would then be plunged into a cauldron of boiling ale in the kitchen below.

The Jarmans dispatched 59 of their guests in this way, allaying suspicions by saying that the victims had left the inn before anyone else was up. Thomas Cole, a wealthy clothier from Reading, was the 60th, and final, victim of the trapdoor device.

When Cole's horse was found wandering in the village, a search was made for him and his body was discovered in a nearby stream – 'Cole's brook', from which the name Colnbrook arose.

The Jarmans tried to flee, but were overtaken and arrested. They both confessed and were hanged in Windsor Forest.

Legends of the Forest

Epping Forest, Essex

THE GREAT Forest of Epping once stretched from Bow in London almost to Colchester in Essex. The forest was declared a royal hunting preserve after the Norman Conquest, and poachers unfortunate enough to be caught there were branded, mutilated or killed.

Within the great forest there were, once, many villages and hamlets, and the villagers had tree-lopping rights. These rights were maintained by a ceremony held every year on 11 November, when the eldest villager would embed his axe in a tree chosen to be 'lopped'.

One year, the lord of the manor tried to prevent the people from exercizing this right. On the day of the ceremony he first invited them to a feast and made them drunk, then he locked the door on them. Rather foolishly, he overlooked the fact that they had brought their axes with them. They chopped down his door, made their way to the forest and carried out the ceremony as usual.

The dark glades of oak, elm and beech provided shelter for vagrants and cut-throats. The notorious outlaw, Dick Turpin, had one of his many hideouts in the forest. His ghost is said to be seen to this day – riding a phantom horse down Traps Hill.

In the 18th century, a clergyman was walking in the forest one day when he was waylaid by an armed robber. Putting his trust in God, he began to sing at the top of his voice, 'Guide me, O Thou Great Jehovah'. The would-be assailant was so startled by this unusual reaction that he turned and fled!

The Hellfire Club

West Wycombe Park, Buckinghamshire

SIR FRANCIS Dashwood, owner of West Wycombe Park in the early 18th century, founded a society called the Knights of St Francis. This secret brotherhood was limited to 24 men of social prominence who met at Medmenham Abbey, near Marlow. Here they conducted mock religious services and held black masses.

Before long, the society became known as the Hellfire Club, with the motto 'Do what you will'. Dashwood had his workmen dig a series of artificial caves in the hillside at West Wycombe, and these were said to have been used by the Hellfire Club for 'unspeakable orgies'.

On top of St Lawrence's Church, opposite the park, is a golden ball which was added by Dashwood as a meeting place for ten of his 'knights'. The caves are now used to house a waxworks display.

*Left and above: The autumn colours of Epping Forest
where, it is said, the ghost of Dick Turpin and his
phantom horse may still be witnessed.
Below: St Andrew's Church, Greenstead, Essex.*

East Anglia and the Fens

The Devil Dog

Blythburgh, Suffolk

DEMON dogs, and uncanny black dogs generally, are common to East Anglia. The 15th century Church of the Holy Trinity at Blythburgh was once visited by the Devil in the form of a black dog, during one of the services.

On Sunday 4 August 1577, a 'strange and terrible tempest' was said to have struck the church. The spire crashed through the roof and shattered the font, killing three members of the congregation and scorching several others. No one doubted this was the Devil's work when his clawmarks were found on the north door, through which he rushed out towards Bungay.

Black Shuck

Bungay, Suffolk

DURING the same wild storm that was attributed to the Devil at Blythburgh, a black demon dog also caused havoc in the church at Bungay. An old pamphlet reported that two worshippers were strangled while praying, and a third was left 'as shrunken as a piece of badly scorched leather'.

In East Anglia this spectral or 'demon' hound is often referred to as Black Shuck. He is a dog that walks alone, loping along river banks and lonely roads. He usually emerges from his hiding place at dusk – and has been seen leaping over churchyard walls and vanishing among the tombstones.

In Suffolk, Black Shuck is considered fairly harmless unless challenged. At Claptown Hall in Stowmarket, however, his appearance is particularly frightening. He is said to be the guardian of hidden treasure, and he has the body of a monk and the head of a hound.

The Norfolk Shuck has much in common with the werewolves that haunted this region in the Middle Ages. He is black as ebony and howls fiendishly. His favourite pastime is padding along behind terrified travellers and breathing hot breath on their necks. Motorists have reported swerving violently to avoid a monstrous black hound as it crosses the road.

The Essex Shuck, on the other hand, is quite a kindly creature – and has even been known to protect travellers on lonely roads. It is only his habit of haunting graveyards that identifies him as a demon dog.

Below: Blythburgh church – once visited by the Devil in the form of a black dog.

Right: Black Shuck, the name given to demon dogs in East Anglia, is most often seen leaping over churchyard walls and disappearing among the tombstones.

The Witchfinder General

Bury St Edmunds, Suffolk

BURY St Edmunds was originally called St Edmondsbury, after the Suffolk martyr St Edmund, who was slain in AD869, and was the last king of the East Angles.

Eight centuries later, 68 people were put to death in the town by Mathew Hopkins, the self-appointed Witchfinder General. Hopkins was an unsuccessful lawyer from Manningtree in Essex. His career took a turn for the better when a woman denounced her elderly neighbour who, while being interrogated by Hopkins, implicated 32 other people. This made him aware of his 'talent' for terrorizing old women.

Any old woman who kept a pet in East Anglia during the 1640s was risking death. After adequate persuasion from Hopkins, a widow of Huntingdon declared that her two pet dogs were her 'familiars', and she was hanged as a witch. An elderly woman from Fressingfield suffered the same fate when forced to confess that her three caged birds had made a cow jump over a stile and immobilized the wheels of a cart.

Hopkins died in 1647. Legend says he was himself accused of witchcraft, tortured and executed – but there is no proof of this.

Right: The ruined walls of Bury St Edmunds Abbey.

Hereward the Wake

Ely, Cambridgeshire

HEREWARD the Wake – meaning the 'wary' – is Fenland's most famous hero. He was a wild youth, and when he was 14 his father persuaded the king, Edward the Confessor, to make him an outlaw and send him abroad.

Hereward returned to England on hearing that the Normans had seized his father's estates. In 1070, he became the leader of a band of Saxon nobles who were holding out against the Conquest from the Abbey at Ely.

When William the Conqueror led his army to Ely, Hereward twice foiled his attempts to build a causeway across the marshes. William then encamped at Brandon to plan his third attempt.

Hereward rode to Brandon, and on the way met a potter whose help he enlisted. The two men exchanged clothes, and the potter lent Hereward his wares. In this disguise he was able to get into William's camp and overhear his plans.

When William built his third causeway and sent his men across it to Ely, they were ambushed and killed by Hereward's men – and the causeway again destroyed. Hereward was eventually betrayed by a chaplain, but it took 20 Norman soldiers to kill him.

Left: Ely, silhouetted against an evening sky.
Above: The impressive interior of Ely Cathedral.

Fenland Legends

The Stilted Army

The Fens

THE Roman invaders used to graze their horses on the lush grass of the Fenlands, and the Fenmen often took advantage of this by ambushing the guards.

A general from Italy's Pontine Marshes had a solution for the Roman soldiers. He trained them in the use of stilts, which made them less vulnerable in the boggy country and enabled them to see their attackers more easily.

The Fenmen were baffled by this for a while – but soon learnt how to knock the Romans off their stilts and stab them as they fell to the ground.

Jack-o'-Lanterns

The Fens

THE Fens are now virtually drained, but in the last century there were still hazardous swamps and bogs. Lone travellers crossing the marshlands at night would sometimes encounter the terrifying Jack-o'-Lanterns – weird, glowing lights that hypnotized those who looked at them.

They were also known as Will-o'-the-wisps, and their ghostly dancing above the swamp-waters would lure travellers to almost certain death in the deep bogs.

In all probability, the lights were caused by small flames – fuelled by the marsh gasses. But to the Fen dwellers they were evil spirits, and the only escape was to lie face downward until they danced away again.

All pictures: The Fenland swamps, now virtually drained, still conjure up images of brooding mystery.

King Canute

The Fens

*H*AVING proved to his flatterers that he was unable to induce the waves to turn back, King Canute was reputed to have wandered off by himself and gone fishing. He was still in his boat, somewhere in the Fens, when dusk fell.

He sought shelter at a monastery, but the drunken monks turned him away – and he found refuge in the hut of a poor fisherman.

The man told him that many years before his wife had been raped at the same monastery, and when he went to her aid he had been beaten to within an inch of his life. His wife had died shortly afterwards, and every year, on the anniversary of her death, the fisherman had killed a monk.

Canute decided that one monk a year was insufficient retribution, so the following morning he ordered his fleet to attack the monastery. A great many of the monks were killed, and those who escaped death were forced to build a new fishing village.

In return for his kindness to the king, the poor fisherman was made its first mayor. Today the village is known as Littleport.

Murder in the Red Barn

Polstead, Suffolk

MANY people thought Maria Marten and William Corder an ill assorted couple. Maria, the daughter of a farm labourer, lived at Polstead; she was 25 years old, attractive and very popular. William, four years her junior, was already a prosperous farmer – but was considered shifty and devious.

Maria became pregnant, but the baby died. Corder had promised to marry her but had not done so, and the couple quarrelled. Maria's parents then insisted that a marriage should take place, and Corder said he would take Maria to Ipswich and marry her there.

Instead, he took her to the Red Barn – a red-roofed building on his estate – where he told her that a horse and gig waited to take them to Ipswich. Maria was never seen alive again.

Corder wrote to her parents saying they were married and living on the Isle of Wight. But Mrs Marten had a vivid dream in which she saw her daughter murdered and buried in the Red Barn.

As a result of her persistence the barn was searched and Maria's body discovered. Corder was found guilty of her murder, and on 11 August 1828 was publicly hanged at Bury St Edmunds.

The 'Feriers'

Stowmarket, Suffolk

THE Stowmarket area was a particular haunt of the fairies – or 'feriers' as they were called locally. It was unusual for them to appear to mortals, but when they were seen they were said to be 'sandy coloured'.

However, a widower who lived at nearby Onehouse declared that their dresses 'sparkled as if with spangles'. He was crossing a meadow on his way home one night when he saw a ring of the 'feriers' dancing in the moonlight.

He noted their gleaming attire, but hurried on – not liking to stop and stare. His courtesy seems to have been well rewarded, for not long afterwards the feriers began to visit him at home.

They came regularly and chopped firewood for him, filling his stove with dry wood every night. They also made him delicious cakes, laughing gleefully as they stirred the mixture. Fairies are particularly fond of making cakes – and are known to be very noisy in the mixing of them.

They warned him never to speak of their visits. But one night he forgot the warning, and boasted about them to his friends at the tavern. He never saw the feriers, the feriers' cakes or the chopped wood again.

All pictures: Not only can Suffolk offer a wealth of interesting places to visit; it also is rich with local legends.

The Fornaby Stone

Caistor, Lincolnshire

ST Paulinus was a 7th century missionary credited with exceptional powers. One day, he was riding an ass along the ancient track that runs near Caistor, when he came upon a farmer sowing corn.

St Paulinus asked the man to spare him some of the grain to feed his ass, but the farmer replied that he had none. Seeing a sack in the field, the saint asked what was in it.

The farmer answered quickly with a lie. 'That is no sack,' he said, 'but only a stone.'

'Then so it shall be!' replied St Paulinus – and the sack was turned to stone. It came to be called the Fornaby Stone and now stands on Fornaby Top. Misfortune is said to befall anyone who attempts to move or damage it.

'Bigger nor a Hog'

Caistor, Lincolnshire

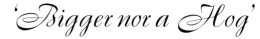

CHURCH Stowe used to be referred to as 'Stowe-Nine-Churches', because it was removed nine times from the proposed site during the building.

The Lord of the Manor chose a hilltop site for it, and set his craftsmen to work. Nine times they laid the foundations for the church – and as many times they found no trace of their labours remained the following morning.

All their tools and materials had also disappeared mysteriously, and after a search they were found on the spot where the present church now stands. So one of the workmen was told to keep watch all night to find out who was moving the stones. But next morning, he could only describe what he had seen as 'summat bigger nor a hog'.

The attempt to build the church on the hill was abandoned, and the present church erected on the site so persistently indicated by . . . who knows what?

Left: A dramatic Lincolnshire sunset.
Right: Lincoln, with its Cathedral towers, suggests an ideal setting for a chilling ghost story.

The Hauntings

Epworth Rectory, Lincolnshire

THE WEIRD hauntings that occurred at Epworth Rectory were never explained, but they were certainly varied. The victims were the Reverend Samuel Wesley – father to the famous John – his wife, servants, and his daughter Hetty.

During the winter of 1715-16, strange howls and groans were heard by the entire household, and an almost continuous banging echoed from the attic.

One night, the Reverend Wesley was awakened by the sound of coins being tipped on to a hard surface. On another night he heard the sound of bottles being smashed.

Several members of the household claimed to have glimpsed the ghostly presence. Hetty said it was a woman in a white gown – but Mrs Wesley considered it looked 'more like a headless badger'.

The Fisherman Founder

Grimsby, Humberside (formerly Lincolnshire)

THE ANCIENT town of Grimsby was traditionally founded by a fisherman called Grim. He had been ordered by the usurper Godard to drown Havelok, the true heir to the Danish throne. But he escaped with the boy to England – and Grimsby.

Havelok later worked for the Earl of Lincoln as a kitchen boy, and there gained a reputation for his skill at sports. Earl Godrich of Cornwall had a ward, Goldborough, who was heiress to the kingdom. Having heard of Havelok's reputation, he decided to marry her off to the kitchen boy so that his own son could be king.

Goldborough took none too kindly to the match, but was forced to marry Havelok or die. Then one night she saw a light shine out of her husband's mouth and a voice told her that he would be king of Denmark and England.

This came about with the help of Earl Ubbe of Denmark, when Havelok's true status was known. Godard was defeated and Godrich burnt for his treachery.

Havelok ruled England and Denmark for 60 years, and Goldborough – having now taken kindly to the marriage – bore him 15 children.

The Boggart Shoemaker

Hob Hurst House, Derbyshire

HOB Hurst's House is a Bronze Age barrow that was the dwelling of a kindly boggart – a sort of goblin – whose kindness sometimes went too far!

A poor shoemaker was unable to earn enough to keep himself and his family, and this distressed him. But one morning he found the leather he had cut out already made into a beautiful pair of shoes.

He sold the shoes that day, and with the money bought enough leather to make two further pairs. The next morning he found that the new leather had also been made into shoes.

This went on and his stock of shoes kept getting bigger. So he stayed up one night to see who was making them – and discovered Hob Hurst at work on the leather.

As soon as the boggart had finished a pair of shoes, the shoemaker put them away. But Hob Hurst worked so fast that soon the little shop was filled with shoes. When there was no more room in the house, the shoemaker threw the shoes out of the window as fast as the boggart could make them.

There is now a common Derbyshire saying that something made too quickly is done 'faster than Hob Hurst can throw shoes out o' t' window.'

Left and below: Colourful Derbyshire landscapes.

Halter-Devil Chapel

Muggington, Derbyshire

THE TINY chapel attached to a farmhouse at Muggington has been given the local name of 'Halter-Devil Chapel'. It was erected by Francis Brown in 1723, in gratitude for an incident that made him give up drinking.

Formerly, Brown had been a very heavy drinker indeed. One stormy night he was due to meet some friends in Derbyshire and his family advised him to abandon the journey, both he and the weather being so intemperate. But Brown swore he would ride there, even if he had to 'halter the Devil' to do so.

He lurched drunkenly out into the darkness to put the halter on his horse – and found that it had grown horns! He was so shocked that he gave up drinking and built the chapel.

The animal he had tried to halter in the darkness was, in fact, a cow.

St Catherine's Well

Newark-on-Trent, Nottinghamshire

ST Catherine's Well, by the river at Sconce Hill, Newark, is where a 13th century knight slew his friend. Both the knight, Sir Guy Saucimer, and his friend Sir Everard Bevorcotes were in love with Isabella de Caldwell.

Sir Everard won Isabella's affections and, in a fit of jealousy, Sir Guy killed him. At the spot where Sir Everard's body fell, a spring gushed from the ground. This was later to become St Catherine's Well, but at the time Sir Guy fled from the scene, overcome by remorse and guilt.

Isabella died from grief and Sir Guy went abroad – where he contracted leprosy. One night a vision of St Catherine appeared to him, saying that the waters of the spring at Newark would cure him.

He returned to England and bathed in the spring – and was indeed cured. From that time forth he led a holy life, and was canonized as St Guthred when he died.

Far left and left: The English Shires, steeped in history and folklore, offer a wealth of curious myths and legends. Right: The 'Trip to Jerusalem' is claimed to be England's oldest inn, and dates from the Crusades.

Mortimer's Hole

Nottingham, Nottinghamshire

THE 'Trip to Jerusalem' is reputed to be one of England's (many) 'oldest inns'. It dates from crusading times and is built into the rock of Nottingham Castle.

A cave, known as Mortimer's Hole, leads from the cellars to the castle, and through this, Edward III is reputed to have crept to capture Roger de Mortimer, his mother's lover.

Mortimer was put to death, and his ghost is still said to haunt the cave.

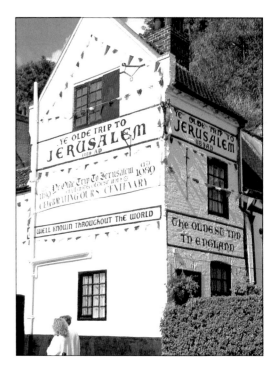

John Tame

Fairford, Gloucestershire

ST MARY'S Church, Fairford, is unique for its medieval stained glass windows. The 'Last Judgement' window depicts particularly vivid scenes of the terrors of hell. The glass was installed by John Tame, a wealthy merchant whose monument is inside the church.

Legend makes Tame a pirate who looted the stained glass from a Flemish ship, and then installed it in the church as atonement for his villainy. In fact, John Tame completely rebuilt the church in the 15th century, and it is much more likely that he imported Flemish craftsmen to make the glass.

Witches at the Crossroads

Fairford, Gloucestershire

FAIRFORD was known for the number of witches who lived there. Maliciously mischievous, they would seize traders on their way to market and imprison them at the Poulton crossroads, holding them there until it was too late for them to sell their wares.

The witches have been dead for years, but some people say they still haunt the crossroads – which is also known as 'Betty's Grave'.

Betty was a local girl who poisoned herself after being crossed in love. Like many suicides, she was buried at the crossroads in order to confuse her earthbound spirit.

Below: A quiet corner of Gloucestershire.
Right and far right: The River Wye and the edge of the Forest of Dean in both summer and autumn livery.

A Gipsy Legend

Forest of Dean, Gloucestershire

THE unspoilt wilderness of the Forest of Dean attracted gipsy families from the time they first came to Britain, early in the 16th century. Ghosts and demons are very much part of gipsy folklore and, according to one legend, even their favourite instrument was the Devil's invention.

A beautiful gipsy girl, Maria, fell in love with a *gorgio* – a non-gipsy – but he did not return her affections. Desperately, she turned to the Devil for help, agreeing to sell the souls of her family to him in return for the *gorgio's* love.

The Devil turned her father into a sound-box, her mother into a bow and her four brothers into strings. From these six souls he created the violin. Maria quickly learnt to play the remarkable instrument and soon the *gorgio* fell in love with her.

However, the Devil had two more souls to claim – and he carried Maria and her lover off to hell. The violin was dropped on the ground where Maria had been playing it, and there it remained until a poor gipsy boy found it. Ever since then it has been the musical symbol of gipsy life.

A Tortured King

Gloucester, Gloucestershire

EDWARD II was not a popular king, but the manner of his murder in 1327 turned him into a martyr. He was tortured to death with a red-hot iron at Berkeley Castle, and almost certainly his queen, Isabella, was involved in the murder.

The abbots of Bristol and Malmesbury refused to accept the king's body, fearing Isabella's anger. But Abbot Tholsey of Gloucester took the body and buried it near the high altar of St Mary's Abbey. It soon became an attraction for pilgrims and the abbey prospered, and was later enlarged into what is now Gloucester Cathedral. Bristol and Malmesbury abbeys, on the other hand, fell into decline.

Edward's splendid tomb in Gloucester Cathedral was raised by his son, Edward III. The face of the effigy is twisted with pain, and is said to have been copied from a death mask showing the king's final moments of agony.

Tailor Mice

Gloucester, Gloucestershire

BEATRIX Potter heard the story of *The Tailor of Gloucester* while staying in the neighbourhood.

The tailor's unfinished suit was stitched for him by a team of industrious elves. Beatrix Potter immortalized the story in her own inimitable way by replacing the elves with mice!

Below, far left: This ancient milestone is set in a drystone wall at Bisley, Gloucestershire.

Below left: A detail from the highly decorative south porch of Gloucester Cathedral.

The Quarrelsome Giants

The Wrekin, Shropshire

THE Wrekin Hill in Shropshire was said to have been made by two quarrelsome giants. They dug the earth from the River Severn, and when they had made the Wrekin they both lived inside it. But being quarrelsome, they each wanted the bigger part.

At first they shouted abuse at each other – which caused some uncommonly high winds to blow round the Wrekin at the time. Soon, however, they came to blows. One struck at the other with his spade, missed, and split the rock now called the Needle's Eye.

He was about to strike a second blow, but a raven prevented him by pecking at his eye. The enormous tear the giant shed formed the pool known as the Raven's Bowl, which never dries up, even in mid-summer.

The quarrel continued, the giant with the spade chasing his companion round and round the Wrekin until both were dizzy, and the whole neighbourhood shook. Then, with a final blow, he knocked the other giant unconscious and quickly imprisoned him in Ercall Hill.

If you should pass that way at midnight, you may still hear the captured giant groan.

Left: The ruins of Much Wenlock Priory, Shropshire.

The Slaughtered King

Dunmail Raise, Cumbria

THE BLEAK road across Dunmail Raise – between Keswick and Grasmere in the Lake District – runs over an historic battlefield. The bones of Dunmail, the last King of Cumberland, are said to rest under the great pile of stones at the summit of Dunmail Raise.

Edmund, King of the Saxons, joined forces with Malcolm, King of Scotland in 945AD. Together they fought, and defeated, the King of Cumberland.

Edmund himself killed Dunmail on the spot where the huge heap of stones lies today. Having slaughtered his enemy, he then ordered his men to collect rocks and boulders and pile them on the king's body, to mark for ever the place of victory.

Edmund then captured Dunmail's two sons and, in an act of needless cruelty, had their eyes put out. The golden crown that had belonged to the last Cumbrian king was cast into Grisedale Tarn on the Helvellyn range.

Dunmail's 'Raise' – the word means a 'heap of stones' – has never been excavated to find the evidence of his historic burial. Neither, for that matter, has his crown ever been recovered from the waters of Grisedale Tarn!

Right: A shaft of sunlight pierces a dramatically darkened landscape in Borrowdale, Cumbria.
Far right: Derwent Water and Ashness Bridge.

King Arthur's Question

High Hesket, Cumbria

A GIANT once had his home in the ancient hill fort called Castle Hewen, near High Hesket. King Arthur, then living at Carlisle, set out to punish this giant for misusing a maiden.

When Arthur reached the magic ground surrounding the castle all his strength left him, and he was helpless. The giant promised he would regain his strength if he could answer the question 'What is it a woman loves best?'

King Arthur asked his knights, and the ladies of his court if they knew the answer – but none of them did. Then one day when he was out riding he met an old hag, and she declared that she knew the answer to the question. Arthur promised her anything she desired, if she would tell him.

The answer was 'Woman loveth her own will best'. In return for it, the old woman wished to be married to one of King Arthur's knights.

The loyal Sir Gawaine, delighted that the king had regained his strength, volunteered to marry the hag. On the night of the wedding an evil spell was broken and the bride appeared as she really was – young and beautiful.

The Ebbing and Flowing Well

Giggleswick, North Yorkshire

NORTH-EAST of Giggleswick is an unusual healing well. It is called the Ebbing and Flowing Well – and that is exactly what it appears to do.

In nearby St Alkeda's Church a 19th century stained-glass window shows the spirit of the well hovering above the water in the form of an angel. This is a Christianized version of the original spirit, a pagan water-nymph.

The nymph was being chased by a satyr – a boisterous creature with the body of a man, the legs of a goat and an insatiable appetite for nymphs. The nymph was fast becoming exhausted and knew she could not outrun this satyr, so she prayed to the gods for help. One of them heard her and turned her into a healing spring of water, which, to this day, ebbs and flows with her panting breaths.

Many hundreds of years later, in the 17th century, a highwayman called John Nevison evaded capture by letting his horse drink at the well. The water gave the horse strength enough to leap from the top of a cliff, and Nevison escaped. The cliff is still known as 'Nevison's Leap'.

Mother Shipton

Knaresborough, North Yorkshire

URSULA Southeil – later to become 'Mother Shipton' – was born in a small cave in Knaresborough in 1488. Her mother died giving birth to her and, at the same time, 'strange and terrible' noises were heard and lightning flashed.

Ursula married Toby Shipton in 1512. Not long afterwards she became renowned – and feared – for her prophecies and predictions. It was said that she foretold the invasion and defeat of the Spanish Armada in 1588, and the Great Fire of London in 1666.

Far left and left: The North Yorkshire Dales.
Below: Tiny objects are turned to stone at the curious Petrifying Well, beside Mother Shipton's Cave.

By now she was called Mother Shipton, and her appearance alone was enough to cast her in the role of a witch. It was said that 'her statue was larger than common, her body crooked and her face frightful.' But there was no denying her extraordinary powers and 'understanding'.

Local curiosity was aroused and prying neighbours became intolerable to her. She is reputed to have bewitched a feast at which most of her neighbours were present, so that they fled from the house pursued by hideous goblins.

Mother Shipton's Cave at Knaresborough remains as her memorial, and beside it is the extraordinary Petrifying Well that appears to turn anything to stone.

The Witches of Pendle

Pendle Hill, Lancashire

LANCASHIRE Hill Country is witch country, and the villages around Pendle Hill are remembered for one of the most infamous witch hunts of the 17th century. On Thursday 20 August 1612, three generations of witches were marched through the streets of Lancaster and publicly hanged about a mile outside the town.

Anne Chattox and Elizabeth Southernes – known as 'Old Chattox' and 'Old Demdike' – had fallen on hard times since their husbands died, and there was an ongoing feud between them. The old women had large families and both were known locally for their acts of 'witchcraft'.

It was Alizon Device, the eldest of Old Demdike's grandchildren, whose action led to the witches' trial and the executions that followed it. Six months previously, on her way to market with her mother's dog, Alizon had met a pedlar called John Law who refused to give her anything. She threatened to curse him, whereupon, much to her surprise, he fell down in a fit.

John Law's son took his now semi-paralyzed father to Roger Nowell, the newly appointed magistrate. Nowell promised that justice would be done, and had Alizon Device brought to him for interrogation.

Whatever methods Nowell used, they were devastatingly effective. Not only did Alizon admit she had put a spell on the pedlar, she also confessed she could speak to animals – including her mother's dog – and admitted that her family

and friends had performed acts of witchcraft. By the end of the day, both Demdike and Old Chattox stood accused of witchcraft and murder.

Demdike, Chattox and Chattox's daughter, Anne Redfearn, were arrested and sent to Lancaster Castle. It was said that Old Demdike was taking her annual bath at the time of her arrest, and was only given clothing when she reached the castle.

At the trial Nowell persuaded Alizon's nine year old sister, Jennet, to give evidence against her

grandmother, her mother, Bessie, and various other relatives.

Old Chattox, Demdike and nine of their relatives were convicted on an extraordinary variety of charges. These included 16 murders, the desecration of graves, communing with evil spirits and plotting to blow up Lancaster Castle by magic.

Chattox shifted the blame on to Demdike, saying the other woman had invited her to a feast with demons and persuaded her to sell her soul to the Devil. But Old Demdike cheated the gallows and died at Lancaster Castle.

Right: The stone ramparts of Lancaster Castle.
Below: The Forest of Bowland, Lancashire.

Robin at Sea

Scarborough, North Yorkshire

SCARBOROUGH has its own legend of Robin Hood. He was said to have joined the crew of a fishing boat in order to help the fishermen. But not being experienced in the ways of the sea, he neglected to bait his hooks before casting them overboard. Needless to say, he contributed nothing to the day's catch.

However, he more than made amends when the fishing boat was attacked by a French man-o'-war. Robin boarded the raiding ship, killed the captain and captured a large amount of gold, which he duly presented to the fishermen.

Above: Colourful fishing boats find the harbour at Scarborough a safe haven.
Right: From its hilltop stronghold, Scarborough Castle overlooks the harbour.

Shrove Tuesday Skipping

Scarborough, North Yorkshire

A BELL ringing from the museum at noon, and all-day skipping matches on the foreshore are ongoing features of Scarborough's Shrove Tuesday celebrations. Some traditionalists maintain that skipping itself dates back to pagan fertility festivals, celebrating the rites of spring. However, it appears that the custom of ball tossing was Scarborough's main spring festival activity in the 19th century and, until 1850, Shrove Tuesday was called 'Ball Day'.

A custom known as 'kissing rings' replaced the ball tossing in 1876. No one was quite sure what this activity entailed – but it was short-lived, and ended in 1881.

The Lambton Worm

Worm Hill, Sunderland, Tyne & Wear

YOUNG John Lambton lived in the Middle Ages and persistently went fishing on a Sunday, although he was warned against it. One Sunday, while fishing in the River Wear, he caught a small fish no bigger than a worm and threw it into a nearby well.

When he grew up he never fished on Sundays, but went to the Holy Land on a crusade. While he was there, the worm in the well grew into a dragon and moved to the River Wear. It grew so big it could coil itself nine times round what is now called Worm Hill. Its appetite was huge and it ravaged the district for lambs and cows – and even children.

John Lambton heard of this and came home to slay the beast. He needed the help of a witch, who demanded that in return he kill the first creature to greet him after he had slain the dragon. He agreed, expecting to be greeted by his dog.

When he had killed the dragon, his father appeared unexpectedly on the river bank. John refused to kill him, and the witch put a curse on the Lambton family from that day forth.

Left: Robin Hood's Bay, North Yorkshire.

Index & Place Names

abbey, 18, 21, 66
animals
  badger, 53
  cat, (Dick Whittington's), 34
  cow, 56
  dog, 76
    Black Dogs, 17, 42, 43,
    Demon Dogs, 42
  hog, 52
  horse, 10, 26, 51, 56, 74
  leopard, 8
  oxen, 72
  stag, 25, 60
  swine, 14
Avalon, 18

ball-tossing, 79
'Beast of Bodmin', 8
Becket, 27
Bevorcotes, Sir Everard, 57
birds,
  blackbird, 61
  jackdaw, 60
  raven, 67
Bladud, 14
Blood, Colonel, 37
Bloody Tower, 36
boggart, 55
Bray, Vicar of, 21

Camelot, 16, 18
cannibalism, 20
castle, 9, 13, 16, 26, 50, 60, 66, 76
cauldron, 28
cave, 18, 19, 28, 57, 75
Chattox, Anne (Old Chattox), 76
Cole, Thomas, 39
Conan Doyle, Sir Arthur, 17, 32, 73
  A Study in Scarlet
  Hound of the Baskervilles
  Holmes, Sherlock, 32
Cook, Nell, 27
Corder, William, 48

crusades, 27, 57, 79

Dashwood, Sir Francis, 40
Demon Dog, 42
Devil, 17, 42, 51, 56, 60, 65, 76
dragon, 31, 38, 79

Excalibur, 8

fairies, 15, 49, 73
fairy ring, 15,
'feriers', 49
Fitzwarren, 34
Friar Tuck, 59

Gawaine, Sir, 71
ghost, 8, 16, 20, 21, 29, 40, 46, 53, 55, 57, 61, 62, 63, 65
ghost ship, 29
giant, 23, 26, 67, 71
Giants' Dance, 23
gipsies 65
Godard, 54
Godrich, Earl, 54
Goldborough, 54
gorgio, 65
Griffiths, Francis, 73

Havelock, 54
Hellfire Club, 40
Herne's Oak, 25
hill-fort, 16, 71
Hob Hurst, 55
Holy Land, 27, 79
Hood, Robin, 59, 78
Hopkins, Mathew
  (Witchfinder General), 44

Ireland, 9
Iseult (Isolde), 9

Jack-o'-Lantern, 46

King Arthur, 8, 13, 16, 18, 71
King Aurelius, 23
King Canute, 47

King Dunmail of
  Cumberland, 70
King Edmund of Saxons, 70
King Edward II, 66,
  Edward III, 57, 66,
  Edward IV, 36
King Henry II, 59
King John, 39
King Lud of Britain, 14
King Malcolm of Scotland, 70
King Richard III, 36
King Uther Pendragon, 13
King William (the
  Conqueror), 45
Knockers, 12
Knucker, 31

Lady Lovibond, 29
Leigh, Molly, 61
Little John, 59

magician, 13, 23, 25
Magna Carta, 39
Mahaut, 27
Marian, Maid, 59
Marten, Maria, 48
Merlin, 11, 13, 23
Merlin's Rock, 11
Monmouth, Geoffrey of, 23
Moonrakers, 24
Morglay, Sword of, 26
Mortimer, Roger de, 57

Nevison, John, 74
Nowell, Roger, 76
nymph, 74

Old Demdike (Elizabeth
  Southernes), 76
Ostrich Inn, 39

Pitt, William, 32
pixies, 32
Pocahontas, 30
Potter, Beatrix, 66
Powhaten, 30

Queen Elizabeth I, 21, 36
Queen Isabella, 57, 66

Raleigh, Sir Walter, 36
Roman, 46, 62

St Botolph, 51
St Catherine, 57
St Guthred, 57
St Paulinus, 52
St Peter, 33
satyr, 74
Saucimer, Sir Guy, 57
'Scavenger's Daughter', 36
Seven Stones Lighthouse, 10
Shipton, Mother, 75
Shipton, Toby, 75
shipwreck, 29
Shonks, Piers, 38
skeleton, 18, 20, 68
skipping, 79
skulls, 68
Smith, Captain John, 30
'smith of kind', 72
smugglers, 10, 24
standing stones, 17, 22
stone circles, 20, 22, 23
Stone of Scone, 33
Strand Magazine, 73

Tame, John, 64
Tholsey, Abbot, 66
treasure, 72
Tristan, 9
Turpin, Dick, 40

violin, 65

well, 74, 75
Wesley, Rev Samuel, 53
Whitehead, Sarah, 32
Whittington, Dick, 34
Wild Hunt, 17
Wish Hounds, 17
witch, 19, 22, 28, 50, 60, 61, 64, 75, 76
Wright, Elsie, 73

PLACE NAMES

Arundel (castle), 26
Avebury (stone circle), 20

Bath, 14
Belvoir (castle), 50
Berkeley (castle), 60
Bisham (abbey), 21
Black Down Hills, 15
Blythburgh, 42
Bodmin Moor, 8
Boston Stump, 51
Brent Pelham, 38
Broomlee Lough, 72
Bungay, 42
Burslem, 61
Bury St Edmunds, 44
Byard's Leap, 51

Cadbury (castle), 16
Caistor, 52
Calgarth, Windermere, 68
Canterbury, 27
Chester, 62, 63
Church Stowe, 52
Clark's Loup, Thirlmere, 69
Colnbrook, 39
Cottingley, 73

Dartmoor, 17
Dore (castle), 9
Dunmail Raise, 70

Ely, 45
Epping Forest, 40
Epworth (Rectory), 53

Fairford, 64
Fenlands, 46, 47
Forest of Dean, 65
Frensham, 28

Giggleswick, 74
Glastonbury, 18
Gloucester, 66
Goodwin Sands, 29

Gravesend, 30
Grimsby, 54

High Hesket, 71
Hob Hurst House, 55

Knaresborough, 75

Land's End, 10
London, 32-37
Lyminster, 31

Mevagissey, 11
Muggington, 56

Newark-on-Trent, 57
Nottingham, 57

Peak Cavern, 58
Pendle Hill, 76
Polstead, 48

St Catherine's Well, 57
St Just, 12
Scarborough, 78, 79
Sherwood Forest, 59
Stonehenge, 23
Stowmarket, 49
Swindon, 24

Tintagel, 13

West Wickham Park, 40
Windsor, 25
Wookey Hole, 19
Worm Hill, 79
Wrekin, The, 67